Strategic Innovator

Implementing Change and Creativity For Solopreneurs and Visionaries

Ric Thompson

Just to say Thank You for Purchasing this Book
I want to give you a gift <u>100% absolutely FREE</u>

A Copy of My Special Report

"Outsource Time"

Go to

<u>www.DoneForYouSolutions.com/OutsourceTime</u>

to Receive Your FREE Gift

© 2014

Table of Contents

Introduction

I want to thank you and congratulate you for buying *"Strategic Innovator: Implementing Change and Creativity For Solopreneurs and Visionaries."*

This book provides very solid basics on business innovation so that you can better understand the role innovation plays in business and to help you find ways to become more innovative in all areas of your business.

After reading this guide, you will understand why innovation is so important to business, how to foster more innovation in yourself and those around you, how to overcome common obstacles to innovation, and why innovation can be the difference between success and failure.

If you are ready to take your business to the next level and blow past the competition, innovation is the key to making that goal a reality. Understanding the different kinds of innovation will allow you to choose where innovation makes the most sense for your business and how best to use it to optimize everything from your business process to your profits.

With the help of *"Strategic Innovator,"* you're on your way to achieving just about anything you can imagine. Thanks again for buying, I hope you enjoy it!

Ric Thompson

What is Innovation and Why Does it Matter?

Innovation is defined by Merriam Webster as the introduction of something new. A new idea, method, or device. The definition isn't nearly as exciting as the concept of innovation.

> *"Innovation is the ability to see change as an opportunity - not a threat"*
> *– Anonymous*

Innovation requires imagination. It requires the ability to see possibilities where others see only blank spaces or even impossibilities. It requires a person to step outside of their boundaries and imagine what can be, what should be, and what must be.

Think back to the last time you really engaged your imagination.

For some that may be stretching back all the way to childhood when purple dragons, bubbles, and playing superheroes were tangible and realistic experiences. For the fortunate few, those who are able to engage their imagination on a regular basis, daydreaming about an incredible future may have happened as recently as yesterday.

However, the majority of people don't spend much of their time dreaming about what could be. They're too busy thinking about what they must do to keep moving forward.

That's certainly a large portion of life. However, amazing things happen when we're able to combine our imagination with the need to move forward in business and our personal lives. That's when true innovation occurs. Innovation is the combination of imagination and business. It results in life-altering changes — not only for business owners but more importantly for consumers.

Think about where we would be today without the talents, imagination, and innovation of the Wright brothers; certainly not taking overseas vacations or flying to Vegas for the weekend.

However, innovation doesn't necessarily mean invention. Innovation can mean taking current technologies and using them in a unique and productive new way. Consider, for example, the iPod, which took digital music technology and packaged it in a very user-friendly manner. Now just about everyone has an iPod – whether they're aged five or fifty.

On a more basic level, consider Martha Stewart. She created a market for crafting and home care. People have been crafting and taking care of their homes for centuries without her magazines or television shows, yet she combined the use of the media, crafting, and home care to create an empire.

Here are some other simple innovations that we use every day, yet at one time they were the cutting edge:

- Polar fleece to keep us warm and snuggly.
- Cell phones to keep us in contact with folks we didn't know we needed to stay in contact with.
- Sliced bread for peanut butter and jelly sandwiches.
- Microfiber-covered furniture that means parents can let pets and children on the couch without panicking.
- Travel coffee mugs that make it easy to take your java with you on the road.
- And don't forget about the wonderful car manufacturers who put the DVD players in the minivans to make those long car trips with the kids a little more bearable.

As an entrepreneur, you have the ability to change the world with innovation. True, innovation can lead to something fun like the iPod, but innovation can also truly change the way we live our lives and even the world around us.

For a great example of the life-changing capacity of innovation, we need only look to BlueSky Designs. By imagining the possibility of being able to go camping if you're in a wheelchair, they came up with tents for people with disabilities. While this may not be something that many of us have to consider, they did and changed the possibilities for disabled people everywhere.

Other examples of changing and improving our world are companies that are at the forefront of biofuel and organic pesticides. Innovation doesn't have to come in the size of Google, Apple, or Sony to change our lives. It can come as a quiet strength that makes its way around the world and changes lives for the better. That's what innovation does for the consumer.

What Does Innovation Mean to You as a Business Owner?

Innovation is your key to being successful long term.

Innovation enables you to stand out rather than just be another business in a blur of similar businesses. Innovation enables you to be the "Purple Cow," the remarkable one in a field of sameness. Let the other businesses compete on price; your business will be able to stand above the others. And you can name your fee because you are one-of-a-kind.

When you're able to create a unique product, service, or customer experience you:

Eliminate the Competition

If you're the only place that markets haircuts to men in a sports-themed environment, as Sports Clips does, then you have no direct competition in the marketplace. If you offer drive-thru coffee shops on every block with Wi-Fi and a unique customer experience like Starbucks does, then other coffee shops will be struggling to keep up with you rather than vice versa.

Broaden Your Reach

Once you begin on the path of innovation, each new product or service offered will branch your business into previously untapped customer segments.

Generate Tremendous Profits and Sustainability

So many small businesses go under before they've ever really gotten their feet firmly on the ground. You'll be far ahead of the crowd and destined for success if you have a clear understanding of the importance of innovation to your business.

Being a business owner means you have the ability to make a significant mark on the world. You have the ability to not only change your own life but also the lives of others. Innovation is one of the tremendously exciting aspects about being a business owner. It brings together the imagination and creative endeavors of great minds with the technology, processes, and marketing strategies to create lasting impact.

What's Your Innovation Score?

Innovation is crucial for business survival. If you're unable to change, evolve, and grow as a business, you'll get left behind. It's as simple as that. Not to worry. When you're done reading this guide, you'll be well prepared to take on the world.

Before we get started, spend a few minutes and take this evaluation based on how your business operates today. You'll retake it again after reading the guide to see where you've improved. It's a great tool to evaluate what you've learned.

On a scale of 1-10 (10 being the highest), rank the current state of your business in the area of innovation for each of the statements below.

I understand the importance and benefits of change and innovation in my business.

1   2   3   4   5   6   7   8   9   10

I understand the psychological trends that can be affecting my business and how to stay on top of them

1   2   3   4   5   6   7   8   9   10

I have systems and processes to make innovation a permanent part of my business.

1   2   3   4   5   6   7   8   9   10

Strategic Innovator

I am comfortable with my ability to innovate quickly

1   2   3   4   5   6   7   8   9   10

I know what purple cows and Imagineering are and how they relate to my business success

1   2   3   4   5   6   7   8   9   10

I know what triggers my own creativity and how to tap into that at will

1   2   3   4   5   6   7   8   9   10

I know what blocks my creativity and when to stop pushing it

1   2   3   4   5   6   7   8   9   10

SCORING

Add up all the numbers you circled._____

Divide the total number by 7

Record your "Innovation Score" here _____

Section 1 - Embracing Change and Psychological Trends

Innovation doesn't just happen for most of us. It has to be encouraged, massaged, and put to the forefront in order to happen. We have to make a point of being innovative. We have to set time aside to brainstorm, to look at trends and data, and to encourage innovation throughout the business.

Where Does Innovation Come From?

Innovation happens when we embrace imagination and change, when we allow ourselves to consider the possibilities, and when we allow our business to capitalize on those possibilities.

The first step in innovation and becoming an innovative business is to embrace change and open the door to the immense possibilities.

Innovation occurs when business owners can think creatively, encourage creative thinking and leadership within their organization, and provide the necessary resources, including staff and measurement tools, to make innovation happen.

Innovation Requires Change

Sometimes the biggest challenge to innovation is dealing with change.

You know the old saying: "the only thing constant in life is change." It's true, and yet we still struggle against it.

However, true innovators are able to embrace change and then capitalize on it.

3M capitalized on glue that wasn't sticky enough for the application it was designed for, and instead came up with their now famous Post-it notes which reside in just about every household, office, and classroom around the world.

The difference between innovation and invention is the effects they have. Invention is creating something new, while innovation is the commercialization of that something new. Invention by itself doesn't get anyone anywhere. For example, a Post-it is a wonderful thing, but until the world knows about it, its only purpose is to fill the needs of the owner.

Innovation therefore doesn't have to be a grand invention; you don't have to invent an airplane or the cotton gin. It can be as simple as enhancing the user experience. For example, Starbucks Entertainment President, Kenneth Lombard, described how an innovative mindset at Starbucks resulted in a whole new way of satisfying its customers through music – a move that was achieved by partnering with major record labels to deliver music as a part of the Starbucks user experience.

Another master innovator is the Whole Foods grocery chain, which capitalized on what they saw as a potential trend toward healthy food and organic lifestyles. Innovation isn't about keeping up with the competition. It is about eliminating the competition and making them irrelevant. If you're the leader of the pack, if you're offering something that no one else is offering, then you don't really have competition.

Understanding What Drives Change

Here's an interesting question. What do you think drives change?

- Trends drive change
- Convenience drives change
- Tragedy drives change
- Politicians drive change
- Money drives change

What do all of these have in common?

People.

The underlying factor behind each and every change that occurs is the people that motivated the change. We drive change. When we see something awful happen, we change policies and procedures to ensure it won't happen again. Take seatbelts, for example. Thirty years ago, no one wore them, and now it's the law.

Another example is the trend for health consciousness, which motivated restaurants like McDonalds to use non-hydrogenated oils, and grocers to offer organic foods.

People drive change.

What does this mean to you as a business owner? It means when you pay attention to what's going on around you, stay on top of trends, technology, and possibilities, and you position yourself to capitalize on change, you may find it possible to be an innovative force in the marketplace.

What Happens to Businesses that Don't Embrace Change?

Quite simply, they get left behind.

An extreme case might be Jan, a fitness coach who doesn't use a computer or the internet. Word of mouth may keep her business going for a while. However, people often use the internet to research, and her competition is sure to be listed on the internet. They may even have products they sell online, books, and a whole toolbox of credibility.

Now Jan might get by with word of mouth customers, but she won't grow her business, and she won't be able to take time off to live her life because she'll be too busy trying to earn enough to get by. It's certainly not a way to live and probably not what she had in mind when she became a business owner.

Embracing Change

Successful business owners embrace change as a means to build business. They capitalize on it to improve systems, to increase profits, and to benefit customers. It's a win-win situation.

Facing challenges presented by change head on is another way to embrace change. Think about the last time you faced a challenge. Maybe it was an unhappy customer, maybe your car broke down, or your computer stopped working. Not fun. However, how you handle a challenge is key to being able to see opportunity.

Challenges and obstacles are opportunities for success. Get excited about them! Try to look at a challenge as an opportunity instead of a hurdle. Passion for change is wonderful because it is contagious. When you're excited about change, the people around you will be too.

Understand that change takes time and planning. However, it also happens very quickly. Sounds like an oxymoron....

Let us explain.

The faster you're able to respond to a challenge or to take advantage of change, the better. We'll talk in section three about how to set up your business to maximize your time response. Make a commitment to evolve. Right now, decide whether you are going to remain in the here and now or if you're going to make it a practice to always look for better ways to operate, take up business opportunities, and find more products or services you can offer your customer.

Accept that change brings controversy and criticism. One of the things true innovators often have to deal with is criticism. There isn't a person out there who hasn't created something wonderful that wasn't doubted, ridiculed, and even completely ignored. What makes these people different is their resilience and their ability to focus on their convictions. Be ready for naysayers, and be ready to ignore them. Confidence in yourself and your decisions will make dealing with change easier.

Knowledge not only helps business owners cope with change, it helps them embrace it. A business owner who seeks knowledge about new technologies, new trends, and new ways of doing things is staying on top of the game. And yes, it is a game – you have competition, right? The one who captivates the consumer's mind and captures their loyalty is the winner. Always learn. Never stop.

*"Learn from others' successes as well as their failures.
Learning and innovation go hand in hand. The
arrogance of success is to think that what you did
yesterday will be sufficient for tomorrow."*
– William Pollard

Innovation occurs when change is embraced and out-of-the-box creative thinking occurs. Of course out-of-the-box thinking doesn't happen naturally for everyone. Sometimes it has to be encouraged. Sometimes we have to kick-start creativity. How you deal with change is the beginning of being a master innovator. Here are some fun exercises to get you started on your path to mastering innovation.

Innovation Challenge #1 - Making Changes

Change is hard. The point of this exercise is to consciously make some changes and see how you respond. Change can be having breakfast when you usually don't, or it can be something large like hiring someone to answer your emails for a week – yikes! This exercise will show you how you deal with change, and it will help you deal with change in the future. It will help put things into perspective.

Change your schedule this week. Add something into your schedule, take something out of your normal routine, or mix it up. Try something new. Once you're able to embrace and become more comfortable with change it'll be much easier to see opportunity and to in fact create opportunity for yourself and your business.

Grab a notebook that you can use as you move through this guide and answer the following questions about this challenge.

What are you changing?

How do you feel about the pending change?

How do you feel after the first day?

How do you feel after the second day?

How do you feel after the third day?

How do you feel when the exercise is over?

Innovation Challenge #2 – Fighting Your Fears

Very few people are 100% comfortable with change. It is important to take a look within yourself and determine if a fear of change is causing you to hesitate in your business. Fear slows down the innovative process. Take a few minutes to consider how you currently feel about change and to identify your fears around change. Don't judge. Change, and the acceptance of it, is a process. We all fall somewhere on the spectrum, which means we can all do with some improvement.

The questions below will help you gain perspective on how you currently deal with change, where it trips you up, and how you can maximize change to the advantage of your business. Grab your notebook, and ask yourself the following questions:

How do you perceive change?

How does change make you feel?

Do you embrace it with enthusiasm, or do you dread it?

What fears come up when you think about change?

When something happens, whether it is a new technology, a cancelled appointment, or a natural disaster, what is your initial reaction?

What do you feel when an employee quits or a customer proposes a revised relationship?

How can you adjust the way you see your situation in order to change your experience of the situation?

Innovation Challenge #3 – Embracing Change

Changing your perception of change is one way to embrace change. Grab your notebook and consider the following questions.

Write down the last time you dealt with a challenge and how you reacted to it.

How do you feel when you think about changes or challenges?

Do you feel excited or frightened?

Do you feel empowered and excited by the possibility of a challenge and by the possibility of change, or do you wish it would go away and things would stay the same?

How do you deal with criticism and doubters?

How can you keep them from deterring you?

How can you be better about keeping up to date on the happenings in and out of your industry?

What do you need to do to stay informed?

Innovation Challenge #4 – Go to CAMP

Grab your notebook and a pen and get ready to do some brainstorming. You're going to CAMP. CAMP stands for:

- Collaboration – Working with others to understand and embrace change.
- Adaptation – Embracing change, and capitalizing from it.
- Motivation – Seeking change.
- Preparation – Being ready for change. Embracing the impossible as possible.

This exercise is the beginning of becoming an innovative leader. It will help you see the opportunities to embrace change and create a truly innovative business. Record your thoughts on the following:

Collaboration

How can you collaborate with others to understand and embrace change? This can be anything from joining a mastermind group to becoming part of an online forum or chat room on your business topic. It's a great way to learn what your customers are thinking and needing, and what your competition is up to.

Adaptation

How can you better adapt to change and capitalize from it?

Motivation

How can you seek out change?

Preparation

How can you be better prepared for it when it happens?

Innovation Challenge #5 – Proactive, Not Reactive

To get started thinking about innovation and focusing on becoming a proactive business rather than a reactive business, you need to work on developing an innovative and proactive strategy. Consider the following, and record your thoughts and the actions you can take for each in your notebook.

Look across alternative industries for ideas. For example, Starbucks looked to the music industry to enhance their customer experience. Sports Clips looked to the sports industry to enhance or actually create their customer experience. The iPod looked to the cell phone industry and created the iPhone. Cirque du Soleil combined the concept of the circus and theatre to create their experience.

What innovations or business practices from other industries might be innovative in your industry?

Redefine your buyer. Cirque du Soleil created an entirely new market to dominate. They combined theater and circus. Both theater and circus fans enjoy and seek live entertainment. They are from generally different demographics, yet with similar psychographics or desires. Combining these demographics and the common desire, Cirque du Soleil created a new market.

Who is your current market, and why do they buy?

Now who is completely outside of your demographic but still has similar hopes, desires, and needs?

And how could you meet their needs?

Complimentary product and service offerings. Think about what happens before and after customers interact with your business. For example, if you own and operate a hair salon, one potential service would be to offer umbrellas to customers, with your business name on them on windy or rainy days. This protects your client's newly cut and styled hair. Use your imagination – that's what innovation is all about.

What happens before a customer comes into your salon?

What happens after they leave?

What can you offer them to fill those gaps?

What can you add to your current product line or list of services to enhance the customer experience?

What happens before your product or service is used?

What happens during its use?

What happens after?

Look at the trends. Trends in society can catch on like wildfire. Regularly take a look at what is happening or is on the verge of happening that could affect your business. We spoke earlier about Whole Foods and how they perceived a growing trend toward healthy eating and healthy lifestyles and opened up large, upscale organic grocery stores around the country before it was a trend. They helped move the trend into action. Starbucks did the same thing. Fifteen years ago, we didn't all have to stop by Starbucks for our coffee each morning. Now they're on every corner.

Another example is Food Network Maven Rachel Ray. Her recognizing that families needed food fast came about in the early 90s, when Domino's Pizza was touting their pizza in a "30 minutes or less" guarantee. She thought, why compromise on taste when you could have REAL food just as fast, and came up with Rachel Ray's 30 Minute Meals. These have made millions, and you'd be hard pressed to turn around and not see something with Rachel's face on it today.

What current trends can you tap into?

What emerging trends look promising?

Where can you learn more about what is trending and what the next trend will be?

What trends might you forecast if you had a crystal ball?

What could the future bring to your industry?

What amazing success is in store for your business?

Function vs. Emotion. Take a look at your products or service. Do you offer a primarily emotional or functional product or service? For example, teeth whitening strips are emotional. They're purchased because people are afraid their teeth aren't up to par. A lawnmower on the other hand is a functional item. Pet id tags are emotional. They're based on the fear that our pet will run away or get lost. Air transportation is functional.

Do you offer a primarily emotional or functional product or service?

If it is emotional, can you add something functional or make it more functional?

If it is functional, can you make it more emotional?

"Take small steps toward innovation and change every day.
* Take one tiny step every day
* Take one small risk every day
* The costs for the changes must be low. No budgets necessary.
This creates momentum in the company that renews the company on a constant basis and makes big innovations easier."
— Jack Swinkels, Technical Solutions BV

Section 2 - Speed and Velocity

"Money likes Speed"
– Dr. Joe Vitale

Have you ever noticed that the decisions you make quickly and based on gut instinct are often right, whereas the ones you debate on for days on end generally end up not working out?

Part of the reason for this is the direct result of trusting your gut and your instincts. When you're certain, things move fast. Speed puts you ahead of your competition. While the others are sitting around tripping over their decision-making processes, you're already in action. You're prepared to bring a new product, service, or customer experience to the market before they've even made a decision.

Speed creates momentum. Consider for a moment the days you get a ton accomplished. Generally they start off very productive, right? You get a ton accomplished because of the momentum you've created from the beginning. The same is true for business and money. As you create the momentum for innovation, it'll keep going and going and going. Imagine the delight in working with people who are constantly coming up with and IMPLEMENTING wonderful ideas to help people! What a fun dynamic to be a part of. What a fun dynamic to create.

Speed lets you zip past your competition. It puts you at the forefront of your industry and opens up a world of opportunities. If you're struggling to keep up with your competition, you're missing all the opportunities because you're generally too focused on just staying afloat. So let's begin by looking at some of the ways you can be the business that is ready to act the moment inspiration is ignited.

Innovation Tools and Resources

When it comes to building an innovative business, it's all about what's under the engine.

"Speed and velocity are two different things. To be able to move quickly, you must take the time to perform the preparatory steps like research and root cause analysis completely. My clients always want to rush through or skip steps, but the innovation only comes from doing the work."
— *Jim Canterucci, author of Personal Brilliance*

Doing the work, as Jim Canterucci says, starts with utilizing the tools and resources you have available.

Customers

Customers are often one of a business's most overlooked sources of information. They can be the key to your next big product, service, or customer experience. Listen to them. Ask them questions.

Surveys are an exceptional way to ask your customers questions. They can be found online or you can hire companies to create customer feedback or surveys. You can send customers an email asking for information, feedback, or even offer an incentive to customers if you're looking for communication.

Here are a few of the thousands of survey services available online:

- http://www.infosurv.com/customer_surveys.htm
- http://www.confirmit.com/solutions/application/customer-satisfaction-survey.aspx

- http://www.surveymonkey.com/
- http://www.questionpro.com/

Market Research

Market research is specific research designed to help you both determine the demand for a potential product or service and to determine if you're meeting the needs of your customers. There are wonderful businesses you can employ to help you with market research. You can do it yourself using basic internet search options, or you can outsource the project. We talk about how to outsource in *"Lead: Strategic Management and Leadership for Innovators and Solopreneurs."*

Brainstorming

Brainstorming frees up your imagination to explore the possibilities. Here are a few wonderful group or solo brainstorming activities. Your job: choose one and brainstorm five possible products, services, or customer experiences for your business.

Brainstorming Exercise #1: Listing.

Make a list of fifty new product or service possibilities for your business. Yep – fifty. This will make you really stretch your imagination. Don't worry, you don't have to implement them unless you want to. The exercise is more for the experience of honing your brainstorming and creativity skills than anything else.

Brainstorming exercise #2: Free write.

Choose one of the items from your list above. You have ten minutes. Do not remove your pencil from the paper or your fingers from the keyboard; whichever you choose, don't stop writing. Now let the words flow out of your brain and onto the paper without judgment. What are you writing about? Five new customer services, products, or customer experiences. If you'd prefer to talk instead of write, speak into a digital recorder for ten minutes. Make sure you have a glass of water because you're not going to stop talking for ten minutes!

Brainstorming exercise #3: Looping.

Start free writing. Pause after a couple of minutes and look at what you've written. Look for a gem that expresses the best observation or statement you've come up with so far and transfer the sentence to the top of a new page. Now, start free writing on that topic. Again, pause after a couple of minutes, and repeat the process. Do this a couple times, and you'll have narrowed your ideas into a few solid ideas you can work with.

Tools and resources for innovation are only as good as the people who use them and the systems in place to make the best use of them. If your business isn't structured to handle the process, innovation will move more slowly at first.

Innovation for Optimization

Use innovation to improve business processes. In order to be able to act fast, your business needs to be able to spot trends, anticipate trends, assess new ideas quickly and create an environment that rewards good ideas with action. This means innovation doesn't just happen as a product or service, innovation can occur in the workplace too.

Being innovative means finding and creating new systems and strategies so that you can move quickly.

In **"Lead: Strategic Management and Leadership for Innovators and Solopreneurs,"** we talk about creating systems for optimal productivity and efficiency. If you haven't read that book yet, it talks about how a system is a protocol for how a particular aspect of your business will operate. For example, a customer service system might answer the following questions:

- What happens when a client calls in?
- What happens if they email?
- What happens if they fax?
- Are there common reasons they contact you?
- Billing issues? If so where do they go?
- Technical support? If so where do they go?
- Product questions? What happens next?
- Need to make an appointment? What happens next?

Internally, systems ensure your business is operating as productively as possible. They increase speed. How you use technology and creative thinking can mean faster, better systems within your company.

Your role in the process is to establish an environment that cultivates innovation by creating systems that make it easy to spot trends, anticipate, assess, and reward. If you're a "solopreneur" right now, something that might slow down the creative process would be the fact that you're doing 100% of the tasks required to run your business. Outsourcing some tasks may free up your time to act quickly to change.

Moving in the Right Direction and Finding your Own Road

The only way to be truly innovative is to go your own way. If you follow the road paved by others, the only thing you'll accomplish is pulling in behind them.

Steer clear of me-too marketing and products. Quite often business owners get stuck in the rut of following the herd instead of finding their own path. To be truly innovative, you must create new market boundaries. For example, consider a fast food burger joint whose primary menu items are hamburgers and French fries.

Now what happens if that burger joint, instead of continuing to offer variations of the same burger, now also offers an organic burger or a veggie burger? They're now appealing to an entirely new market previously untapped by their customers. They're widening their customer base by not only appealing to the true junk foodies, but also through their organic and healthy option, to the growing trend of health conscious people. Plus, some of their current clients may have actually been looking for healthier options.

Don't try to be all things to all people, but DO try to innovate as best you can.

Chick-Fil-A is a fast food establishment that is famous for its fried chicken sandwiches – in fact they claim to have invented the chicken sandwich. To tap into the trend toward healthier eating, they added grilled chicken sandwiches and salads with grilled chicken, but they DIDN'T add burgers or hummus and bean sprouts. They stayed consistent with their core message, but still innovated with the trend.

Perfection Hinders Innovation

"Don't worry, be crappy"
– #2 in the 9 Truths of Innovation by Guy Kawasaki.

The theory behind this isn't to intentionally deliver a crappy product, but the point is to not wait until it is perfect. NOTHING is perfect, and if you wait until your product or service is perfect, life and profits will pass you by. Besides, it doesn't really matter what YOU think about the product, your CLIENTS will tell you how they want it. They can't DO that until they are able to try it.

If you act quickly, you can test, modify, and improve your product or service as you receive feedback from consumers, be making money at the same time, and gain market share. See how it is important to create a business that is continually evolving? Introducing a product or service isn't enough. You need to be there constantly improving your offerings and creating new ones. It's exciting to live in a world of creative wealth!

Allow innovation from your customers. For example, if you create a product meant for one thing and people use it differently, embrace that new use. MySpace was meant to target Friendster customers who were tired of paying a subscription fee. What they didn't expect was that the independent musician crowd would be one of their earliest and biggest customer groups. Did MySpace frown and ignore this group? Nope, they smartly embraced them and added more features to their social networking site to make the user experience more beneficial for independent musicians.

Real-time Visibility

Moving quickly means more than just making decisions and getting a product to market quickly. It means telling the world about your innovation. If your market is unaware of your product or service, then it'll fall flatter than big hair in a rainstorm. Utilize the following to get the word out fast:

Technology

Getting the word out about your innovation is key to both testing the waters and to making it happen. For example, Apple leaked bits and pieces about their iPhone for months before it was released. The leaks served to both build hype and, to a certain degree, to test demand. They created a buzz and listened to what their market was saying.

New Marketing

New markets require new marketing strategies. Cirque du Soleil cannot market their show like a traditional circus. That would be like marketing filet mignon to an elementary school. The kids might like it, but the company can't sell at the right price point, and the kids aren't the decision makers with the money.

The burger joint probably can't sell their organic burgers with their big and greasy ad campaign either.

New products and services, and new markets, need new marketing.

Don't Get in Your Own Way

Quite often, business owners can get in the way of themselves. Often our speed problems come from a need to be perfect, insecurity, too much structure, and even too little structure. The ability to move fast comes from several key ingredients:

- You must not expect perfection. Nothing is perfect. Perfection is a process, not an end result.
- You must be confident – despite the naysayers.
- You must walk a tightrope of structure and creativity. Structure can absolutely speed up the process from idea to product. However, structure can also dampen creativity.
- You must understand that innovation is a process, not a single ribbon cutting event.
- You must LISTEN to your market and give them what they want.
- You must have the confidence to create your own market, and not ride the tails of others.
- You must own and control the primary technology in everything you do. If there's a better technology available, use it no matter if anyone else is not using it. Be the first, and make it an industry standard.

This rule doesn't just apply to technology-based businesses. It can apply to anything. For example, if you own a hair salon, controlling the primary technology may mean staying one step ahead of coloring technology and trends. Maybe it means offering customers an entirely different experience, such as offering a concierge service while they are being pampered. It means creating a market and staying on top of it no matter what your business is.

Innovation is about moving quickly. It is about letting go of your fears, conquering them, and confidently embracing ideas that will benefit your customers and your business. Not only do your internal emotions affect the speed of innovation, external factors influence it too. Take advantage of resources, technologies, and systems to move innovation to the forefront of your business. Then and only then can you begin to capitalize on creativity.

Innovation Challenge #6 – Think Fast

In order to stay ahead of your competition, you must be faster than them. Every single one of your competitors has the potential to beat you to the proverbial punch. Smart business owners are always thinking. It's the best way to stay one step ahead of your competition. This exercise will develop your habits around speed and innovation.

Consider the following, and record your thoughts and possible actions you can take in your notebook.

Anticipate.

What will you do to anticipate customer needs, new consumer markets, and better customer experiences?

Assess.

How will you assess ideas for their viability?

How will you know if an idea is a good one or not?

Create an environment for speed.

What in your current business slows down the creative process?

What supports a fast, creative process?

Spot trends quickly.

What business systems are currently in place to spot trends quickly?

Use prototypes and role models.

Find relevant role models and prototypes for innovation. For example, the book *Blue Ocean Strategies* by W. Chan Kim and Renee Mauborgne offers a plan and series of systems and strategies for creating innovation.

Where can you find good system role models?

Innovation Exercise #7 - Test Yourself

Here you're really going to push your own comfort and confidence boundaries. Only when you really push your boundaries can you know what you're truly capable of. The push may result in tremendous innovation, creativity, and an energy that you can use to tap into when you're building a business. Ready?

Record the answers to these prompts in your notebook.

List three targets you have for yourself or your business. It can be something like getting your website up and running, writing your brochure or sales letter, or getting your first sale – anything really.

Write down how long you think it will take you to reach each target.

Now cut that time in half. Yep, half. If you thought it would take you a month to get your website up and running, you now have 15 days. Challenge yourself and get it done.

Section 3 - Purple Cows and Imagineering

Have you ever seen a purple cow? What about an elephant sitting in a tree? A child flying by? Probably not. What do these things have in common? They're certainly unusual. One might say they're remarkable.

Seth Godin, author of *Purple Cow: Transform Your Business by Being Remarkable,* suggests that, "We have now moved into an era where markets are largely satisfied," meaning everyone has everything that they need. He states, "To be noticed in any industry, a product and its marketing need to be remarkable to be seen at all, let alone to sell." A product needs to be as remarkable as a purple cow.

Imagineering on the other hand brings together two key words – imagination and engineering. Imagination is the spark of innovation - the engineering and technology make it possible. If you've ever been to Disneyworld or Disneyland, you've seen imagineering at work. It is the process responsible for taking all of those fantastic stories and turning them into real, tangible experiences that delight kids of all ages.

Walt Disney imagined a theme park where people could come to have fun with their families and explore something completely different from their reality. He used many levels of engineering: civil, automotive, computer, and so on, to bring it all together into an amazing place that has endured the test of time.

Now don't freak out. We're not suggesting that you need to go create a multi-billion dollar theme park next week. What we ARE saying is a business which combines the power of imagination and technology can make anything happen. You can make anything happen for your market and your business.

Here's another definition of imagineering from Tom Attlee of the Co-intelligence Institute. Atlee says Imagineering has three elements:

- Story
- Vision
- Guidance

The story is where you place yourself in the shoes of your potential customer and sense what they feel, deal with, and how they might react to your innovative product or service. A story is the beginning of the creative process because it starts inside you and utilizes your imagination. Much like when you were a child and played pretend, with a story you step into the role of your customer. Who are they? What do they need from you?

Vision incorporates the power of what could be. Now you get to play pretend in the future. What does the future look like? What is your role in that future and what does your customer need from you? Now you're combining what is and what could be.

Combining that with Disney's definition of using technology and engineering to tell a story, we get to the meat of the creative process. Let's step back for a minute and consider three purple cows, three truly remarkable products that have caused a stir and generated tremendous profits as a result of business imagineering.

Spanx

Sara Blakely had an idea one day while sitting on the couch watching Oprah. Oprah commented on how she cut the feet off of her hose because she wanted the control but didn't want the feet to show. Sara didn't pause to dwell on her spark of an idea, she ran with it. With great speed she designed a pair of control garments without feet and hit the road to see who could help her bring her idea to life. Typical of many remarkable ideas, she hit many roadblocks, but Sara KNEW her audience was there, she just needed to find them. Spanx has been featured in more than a dozen feature magazines as well as on Oprah. Blakely recorded more than 150 million in sales in 2006.

One thing Blakely has continued to do, which many business neglect, is that she has continued to offer innovative products. She's kept the momentum going.

VeriChip Pet ID Chips

VeriChip pet ID chips are also a purple cow. The technology used to produce the chips had been around for a while, since 1979, and zoos had adopted the technology to track their animals. It wasn't until VeriChip ran with an innovative ID that the Pet ID chip came to the mass market. Using innovative technology, they found a new market for the product, pet owners, and created a standard of practice for many veterinarians and human societies all around the country. They now project 1 billion in worldwide sales. Pretty profitable innovation!

AeroGrow

Similarly, hydroponics, or the science and practice of growing without soil, has been around for decades. However, the practical application of being able to grow a salad on your kitchen counter in a beautiful and easy-to-use device hasn't. AeroGrow is a remarkable product because it created an entirely new market. Now anyone, absolutely anyone, can grow their own food in their own home. This idea has been so successful that AeroGrow have announced that they've shipped more than 400,000 AeroGardens and more than one million seed kits.

So you see, you don't have to walk on the moon or bring about world peace. Innovation can be as simple and remarkable as a pair of cut-off panty hose!

Theories of Innovation

There are actually several forms of innovation, and we've been talking about them interchangeably. Understanding the theories will help you understand how to fully maximize your business and take advantage of all opportunities. For example, breakthrough innovation is coming up with an entirely new product or service, and when combined with incremental innovation, that breakthrough product can stay on top without any competition.

Let's look at the basic types of innovation.

Breakthrough Innovation

Also called radical innovation, breakthrough innovation is the introduction of an entirely new product or service that is previously unavailable on the market. AeroGrow is an example of breakthrough innovation.

Open Source or Open Innovation

Open source innovation happens when a company collects resources from outside companies. For example, the research and development can be obtained from someone, the patent for a product could be purchased from someone else, and so on. Pharmaceuticals are classic examples of open source innovation. Pharmaceutical companies buy the research from universities, patent medications, and then market them to the public.

Incremental Innovation

This means gradually changing or adding to a product or service. This is basically evolution, and it must occur along with breakthrough innovation. They can exist side by side. For example, the AeroGrow now offers a Classic model, a Professional model, and a mini AeroGrow.

Process Innovation

Similar to incremental innovation, process innovation involves improving a product or service. However, process innovation means offering a significant improvement to a product and capitalizing on it, such as "The New and Improved...." For example, Apple recently released a new and improved version of their iPod. Software companies do this all the time, and even cosmetic companies are frequently releasing new and improved shampoo, mascara, and so on.

And don't forget new and improved food items like Campbell's Tomato Soup or New and Improved Lucky Charms.

Business Model Innovation

This type of innovation involves changing the way your business is conducted. For example, a strictly retail business which operates on a basic product for cash exchange can begin to offer consulting services and change or modify their business model. For more on business models, check out our Business Strategy Guide.

Marketing Innovation

Innovation here means the development of new marketing methods including improving product design, packaging, product promotion, or even pricing. For example, the soda industry is famous for adding new shaped or sized bottles to their product line. You can now get soda in everything from a tiny 6 oz can to a 3 liter bottle.

Differentiation and Remarkability

> *"Discovery consists of looking at the same thing as everyone else and thinking something different."*
>
> *Albert Szent-Gyorgyi*

Part of creating a remarkable product is the ability to see things differently than everyone else. While some people walk around with an innate ability to see the world differently, the rest of us just see what's around us. A true innovator can look at the pen on your desk and see the instrument that can topple governments, solidify dreams, and change the world. The rest of us probably just see the thing we sign checks with.

The key is to occasionally force ourselves to get outside of our proverbial mental box.

Oh, to live in a world where purple cows and imagineering are everyday occurrences. Where business strives to be the best it can be. Where it strives to offer unique and beneficial products and services, life-changing products and services. Where creativity and innovation move at the speed of light and are rewarded with pride, pleasure, and profits for everyone. It is possible to create such a business; many have. Use what you've learned in this section to make your business, and the world, a better place.

Creative Tools to Test Your Limits

As we discuss innovation, purple cows and imagineering, you might be thinking, "Oh God, are all these necessary to create a truly successful business?"

Relax, you don't have to do EVERYTHING, just introduce a great product, service, or customer experience, constantly strive to improve it, create new marketing tools and strategies to spread the word, and foster an environment where innovation is a standard of practice.

Okay – enough with theories and definitions. Let's put them to the test and have some fun!

Innovation brings about change, and change implies risk. We've talked about being comfortable with change in Section one. Let's see what you've learned!

Innovation Challenge #8 – Flex Your Muscles

Roger von Oech offers an exercise that allows you to "flex your risk muscle". In this exercise participants are asked if they hit the Bull's-eye every time. Then they are told, that if so, then you're standing too close to the target. The lesson here is that if you're not failing every now and again, it's a sign you're not being innovative. Everyone has a "risk muscle." The way you exercise that muscle is by taking chances and trying new things. Like all muscles, if you don't use your risk muscle, you lose it.

Think of things that make you uncomfortable, a little beyond your comfort level. For example, if you detest collecting past due money from clients, and you have a client who owes you money, flexing your risk muscle may be to call that client and ask what's up.

Make a list of ways you can flex your risk muscles in your notebook. Then, assign one action you can take for each as a way to keep those muscles in shape.

Continually flexing your risk muscle will result in greater confidence for the big things like jumping on a fantastic idea that came to you while you were at the dentist. Remember, money likes speed, and if your risk muscle is strong, you'll be confident enough to act quickly and not let doubt slow you down.

Innovation Challenge #9 – Creative Thinking Style

What is your creative thinking style?

The point of this exercise is to help you tap into your creative side and learn how to focus on it so you can access it and utilize it when you need to.

Grab your notebook and answer the following questions and prompts.

When do you feel most creative?

Is it when you're working out?

When you hear music?

When you attend a conference or seminar, or maybe when you're playing with your pets or children?

Many things can stimulate creativity. Pay attention to them. Noticing creative moments can become a good habit.

What inspires creativity in you? Music works quite well for some people, others are inspired by problems, and yet others simply by reading about the adventures and successes of others.

How do you best express your creative side? Everyone has a creative outlet, even if they're unaware of it. Think about what works best for you.

Do you communicate better talking, writing, or drawing? Many people use a digital recorder to record their thoughts simply because that's how they best express themselves.

What hinders creativity? Some business owners thrive in busy, noisy environments; others need silence and peace to tap into their imagination.

What gets in the way of being creative? Knowing this, and naming it, will help you eliminate it.

When do you feel least creative? For example, some people are more creative in the morning while others require at least three cups of coffee before the synapses start firing.

Do you generally work better in groups or alone?

Innovation Challenge #10 – Practice Innovative Problem Solving

Here is the final exercise for this section, courtesy of Marshall Thurber. Marshall is world-renowned scholar and futurist whose students include such well-known, successful, business people as: Jack Canfield and Mark Victor Hansen of Chicken Soup for the Soul fame; the founder and creator of Paul Mitchell hair products; Ben Cohen, co-founder of Ben & Jerry's ice cream; Spencer Johnson, author of *Who Moved My Cheese*; Tony Robbins; Harv Eker; and Robert Kiyosaki (author of *Rich Dad Poor Dad*).

This is a big one, so you'll want to give yourself several hours to complete it. You will also need to put together a small team of people to help you with this process – no more than four or five – you don't want this to get unruly. Team members can be employees, associates, or you can bring in one or two other "advisors." You will need a space big enough for everyone to congregate, Post-it notes, and writing implements for everyone.

When you've finished with this exercise, you'll not only have questions answered about how to resolve your biggest issue, but you'll also have the beginning of a solution.

To start, take the biggest issue you are facing right now, and write it down in your notebook. You will use this to create the key question below. Then, assemble your team and following the steps outlined below.

Step one: Create the key question. (An example would be: What are all the key issues that need to be addressed in order for XYZ Company to become [whatever the goal is]?)

Step two: Pass out Post-its to all members of the team.

Step three: Using five to nine words, list all issues related to the question. Write one issue per Post-it. Each issue will start with "We must" and should include at least one action verb and one noun.

Examples:

We Must Maintain Our Integrity

We Must Realize a 15% Profit Margin

We Must Respond to Customer Service Requests within 12 hours.

Step four: Assign a numerical value to each issue. You have 50 points in total to disperse between all issues. Not all issues have to have a numerical value.

Step five: Post the issues on the wall.

Step six: Arrange the Post-its in like categories. Do not talk; this is important. You'll feel a silent synergy and energy running through the group.

Step seven: Evaluate whether everyone is aligned. If they are not, go back, and repeat step six. If they are, move forward to step eight.

Step eight: Create six to ten main category headers that summarize your categories, each header gets it's own Post-it.

Step nine: Evaluate whether any of the categories can be combined. If they can, create a new category heading for those combined categories.

Step ten: If categories cannot be combined, collect all category headings and rewrite each with a super heading.

Step eleven: Now associate two headers at a time and come to a resolution by comparing one to the other and seeing which one "drives" which. (Example: In the process of getting up in the morning you have 2 headings, "Getting up" and Setting the alarm". In this scenario Setting the Alarm, drives Getting up – without the alarm being set, it's highly unlikely that you'd get up on time.) NO compromises are allowed here. There must be a resolution.

Step twelve: Count the number of ins and outs for each header. In the example above since "Getting Up" is diven by "Setting the Alarm," "Getting Up" has an "in" and "Setting the Alarm" has an out. This of it in terms of cause and effect. Causes are "outs" and "ins" are effects.

Step thirteen: Rank the categories and total the predicted points for each. The more "outs" i.e "causes," the higher the rank – so the MOST important thing would have the most number of outs, followed by the next highest number of outs, followed by the next, and so on. These higest ranked categories become your Main Drivers.

Step fourteen: Create a specific plan for how to address each of your main drivers. To wrap it back around, you're creating a plan to address each of the main areas that will "cause" you to reach the objective you stated as the question in Step One.

Take a look at the flow chart to see how the clarity process looks and works.

Marshall Thurber's Clarity Experience - Process Flow

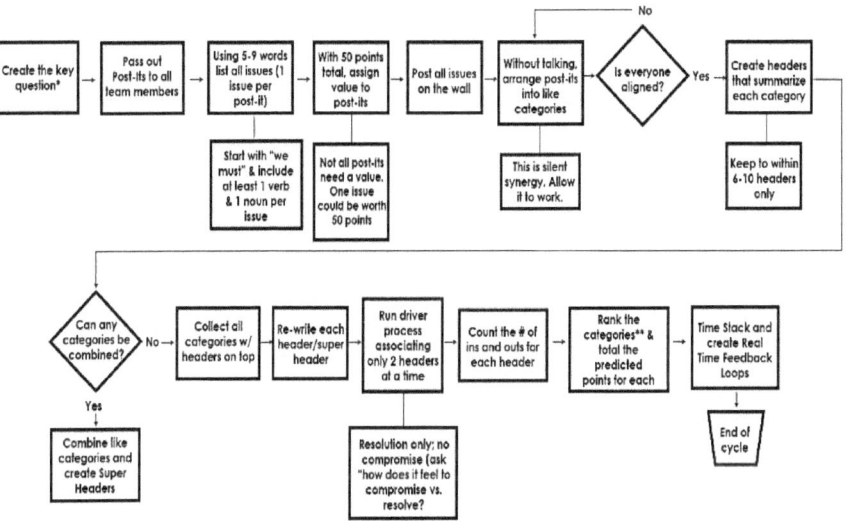

Working Definitions:
*Key Question Sample - What are all the issues that need to be addressed in order for XYZ to become the highest quality and most profitable company in its domain?
** Category Ranking: The number of outs determines the rank i.e. the greatest number of outs is the #1 Driver

Section 4 - Think and Grow Rich

Think and Grow Rich is a book written by Napoleon Hill and originally published in 1937 by the Ralston Society. To this day it is still considered to be one of the premier books on how to attain success. *Think and Grow Rich* has sold consistently since it was first published. According to one publisher, the book has now sold more than 30 million copies worldwide. *Think and Grow Rich* has been on the BusinessWeek Bestseller List for 22 months as of April 2007. The book contains 13 principles to attain success – to think and grow rich.

These principles or laws of success are the foundation for many personal and professional development programs. In Hill's book, the fifth law of success is the law of imagination, or the workshop of the mind.

The Power of the Mind

Napoleon Hill suggests there are two types of imagination: the synthetic imagination and the creative imagination.

The synthetic imagination allows you to arrange old concepts, ideas, and plans into new combinations. It doesn't create; it reassembles already existing knowledge into new forms. It brings together the Coca Cola and the Cherry Cola and gives us Cherry Coke. New products evolve and new methods of doing things are created. However, they are based on already existing knowledge and information.

The creative imagination runs on inspiration. It is fueled by sparks of creativity that hit you when you're in the shower, waiting in traffic, or maybe watching Oprah like Sara Blakely, creator of Spanx. All new ideas come from the creative imagination.

Creativity is the first step in innovation. Without creativity, there would be no ideas to move forward into products and services. However, creativity alone cannot get the job done. Creativity needs structure. It needs organized planning to become innovation.

Organized Planning

The next step in Napoleon Hill's laws of success is the law of organized planning. This is where imagination and engineering meet. This is where story, visualization, and guidance come together. This is where your creativity or the strength of your creative team and your strategies, processes, and resources come together to make innovation happen.

Hill calls organized planning, "the crystallization of desire into action." It's where you make your idea a reality. One of the best ways to accomplish this is to put together or join a team of like-minded people. People who each have their own businesses and reasons for being in a group. This is called a mastermind group.

Mastermind Groups

A mastermind group is a group of like-minded individuals who meet on a regular basis to motivate, inspire, and encourage other group members. The dynamic of a mastermind group benefits members by holding members accountable for setting and achieving their goals. It creates an environment of creativity and innovation. It offers support and answers or potential solutions to problems you're facing, and it enables you as a business owner to help other business owners achieve their dreams and goals.

Why Join a Mastermind Group?

The benefits are so numerous that it is a step that cannot be skipped. Mastermind groups help you widen your vision. The other members will bring new ideas and outlooks into your group, opening up a world of ideas that may never come to you any other way. Mastermind groups hold you accountable for your goals. They don't let you slack off. Mastermind groups enable you to contribute and to receive the benefit of other members' experience.

Mastermind groups keep you inspired to be better, both personally and professionally.

What to Look for in a Mastermind Group

Look for members who are at least as experienced as or more experienced in business than you are.

Look for members who have the right motivations or similar motivations as you.

Look for a group that meets regularly.

Look for a group that focuses on the things you'd like to focus on. There are all kinds of mastermind groups including religious or spiritual groups, personal groups, and business focused groups.

Look for a group that communicates effectively. Not all mastermind groups are good ones. Visit the NOBS student forum, and you'll find a number of like-minded people to connect with and learn from.

Overcoming Innovation Obstacles

Before innovation can happen, before imagination and organized planning are even a possibility, there are key elements of an organization that have to be in place. If they're not, there will be strong barriers to innovation, hurdles you just cannot leap or go around. Let's take a look at them individually.

Keeping Up the Momentum

We've talked about the process of becoming an innovative business, a leader in your industry, throughout this guide. Becoming a leader means finding new and creative ways to create market demand. Stretching your imagination as a person and a company is the best way to get started. To keep the momentum going, challenge yourself. Here are some ideas on how you can challenge yourself to keep the momentum up.

- If you're a solopreneur, challenge yourself to come up with a new idea monthly, quarterly, or on a timescale that meets your business goals.

- Join a mastermind group to broaden your horizons and your possibilities.

- If you have employees, establish an environment that supports innovation.

- Offer contests, hold company meetings, set up a system of financial reward for innovations that are brought to fruition. Wal-Mart is a great example of a company that rewards innovation. They motivate employees to innovate by rewarding employees who have successful ideas (ideas that are implemented and that save or make the company money) with a percentage of the savings or profits. Financial incentives are a great way to motivate! You can bet there is LOTS of innovation going on in that company! Positive and creative environments are fantastic places to work, so you'll not only be creating an innovative business and workplace – you'll be creating an environment that people enjoy being a part of.

Maintaining Marketing Buzz

At least 80% of innovation is getting the word out about your wonderful new product or service. Keep the buzz going about your company with regular press, publicity, and a marketing campaign that keeps your company at the forefront, ahead of your customers. It's the best way to keep the eye on your company and to keep your business motivated.

To think and grow rich, you must first begin with a desire to do so and a faith that you can accomplish the goals you've set for yourself and your business. Along your road to success, you'll master innovation by tapping into your creative mind. You'll not only accept change, you'll embrace it. Change drives innovation and innovation drives change. It's a powerful process, and when you put yourself in the game, when you position your business as a leader in your industry, amazing things can and will happen.

Innovation can be tremendously profitable, and it can also be fantastically rewarding. Purple cows are remarkable. Your products and services can be remarkable too.

Tapping into your creative mind and harnessing your resources like your customers, market research, and mastermind groups are only the beginning. Strategizing and organized planning can be just as exciting. It's like Jack planting that magic bean, watering it, and watching the beanstalk grow up into the clouds, taking him to whole new worlds he could never have imagined.

To your success!

Innovation Exercise #11 – Mastermind Selection

Before you consider joining or creating a mastermind group, it is important to consider what you bring to the group and what you expect to get from it. Consider the following questions and prompts and record your thoughts in your notebook. This will help you find the right group for you.

What do you want from your mastermind group?

What skills, knowledge, and backgrounds do you want your mastermind members to have?

It may be tempting to join a group where everyone has the same or less experience in business than you do. However, consider the advantages of participating in a group where the members are more knowledgeable than you.

Of course, you also have to bring something to the group. What skills, experience, and knowledge can you bring to a mastermind group?

Now, find a mastermind team, based on your criteria laid out in the previous exercise, and join them.

Innovation in Action

Here's where we pull it all together and put it into action. This is the true test of your can-do attitude. How innovative are you? Are you really ready to make your business everything it can be? Take some time, just a bit, and create inspired-action SMART Plans. Then, just before you finish and check reading this guide off of your to-do list, repeat the evaluation you took at the beginning. Taking one look back at all you've accomplished will give you a great feeling.

Go back through your notes and your responses to the exercises and list all of your targets, goals, and action steps. Then answer the following from your responses.

- What target markets are you going to pursue?
- How are you going to pursue change?
- How are you going to stimulate innovation?
- What are you going to do to embrace change?
- How are you going to stimulate creativity?
- What are you going to do to increase your comfort with risk?
- How are you going to ensure that innovation moves quickly?
- What work are you willing to do to make innovation happen?
- How will you use your resources to stimulate and optimize innovation? Etc.

List one item per line, and after you have them all listed, rank each one in order of priority. Rank the one that will make the biggest impact in your business and your life RIGHT NOW as number 1, the second as number 2 and so on down the list.

Take the top three and create a SMART Plan for each one. Work those plans until you hit the target, then come back and create SMART Plans for the next three. Remember, a SMART plan must be:

S – pecific

M – easurable

A – ttainable

R – ealistic

T – ime Trackable

What's Your Innovation Score NOW?

When you've completed this evaluation, compare it to your results the first time you took it. You may be surprised how much you've changed in the short time it's taken you to complete the guide.

On a scale of 1-10 (10 being the highest), rank where you stand now in business innovation.

I understand the importance and benefits of change and innovation in my business.

1   2   3   4   5   6   7   8   9   10

I understand the psychological trends that can be affecting my business and how to stay on top of them

1   2   3   4   5   6   7   8   9   10

I have systems and processes to make innovation a permanent part of my business.

1   2   3   4   5   6   7   8   9   10

I am comfortable with my ability to innovate quickly

1   2   3   4   5   6   7   8   9   10

I know what purple cows and Imagineering are and how they relate to my business success

1   2   3   4   5   6   7   8   9   10

I know what triggers my own creativity and how to tap into that at will

1   2   3   4   5   6   7   8   9   10

I know what blocks my creativity and when to stop pushing it

1   2   3   4   5   6   7   8   9   10

SCORING

Add up all the numbers you circled._____

Divide the total number by 7

Record your NEW "Innovation Score" here _____

Did you see an improvement in your score? Why do you think you did or did not?

Come back in a month, six months, or even a year, and retake the assessment to see how your new understanding of business innovation has changed your business outcomes and your attitude about how innovative you are and how innovative you want to be.

Conclusion

Congratulations on deciding to invest in making your business a master of innovation!

This book provided you with valuable insights into understanding innovation, how it can be used to differentiate your business from the competition, and how you can encourage and create a mindset of innovation in all you do. You learned:

- What innovation is and why it matters
- How innovation can boost your business
- Where your business is right now in terms of innovation
- The relationship between creativity and innovation
- How change and innovation go hand in hand
- How to embrace change in order to build a more innovative business
- How to use creative thinking to open the door to innovation
- The importance of speed to innovation
- Why perfection and innovation are incompatible
- How to use innovation to optimize your business process and systems
- How to overcome common obstacles to innovation
- How to create a SMART plan to turn your innovation inspiration into action

Now it's time to take what you have learned and make a difference in your business. Remember, innovation is the key to the future, embrace it!

Ric Thompson

Check out Ric's other books!!

http://www.amazon.com/dp/B00I3Q2QPK

http://www.amazon.com/dp/B00LIGKRCG

http://www.amazon.com/dp/B00H4HHY56

http://www.amazon.com/dp/B00L9K6928

http://www.amazon.com/dp/B00O170KBC

http://www.amazon.com/dp/B00NRVWE3A

http://www.amazon.com/dp/B00O170KVC